Make sure it's right

Remember to sit properly at your desk when you write.

Hold your pencil lightly in the correct way.

Let your pencil point along your arm.

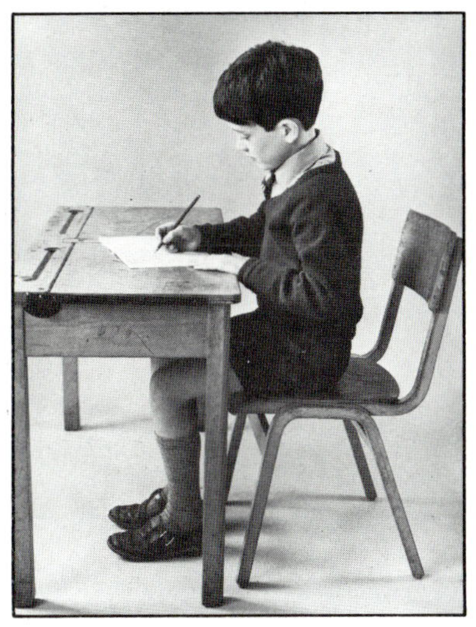

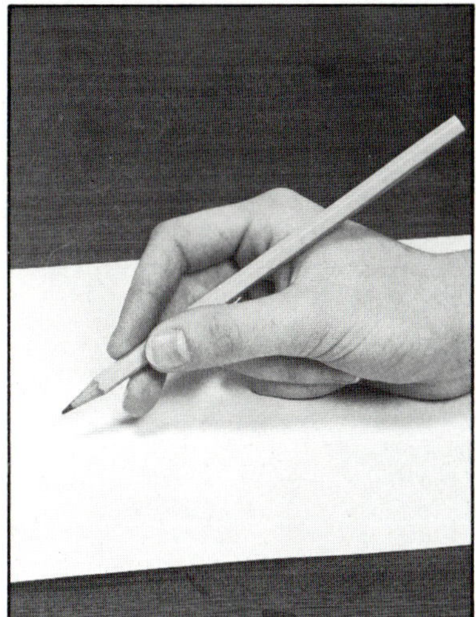

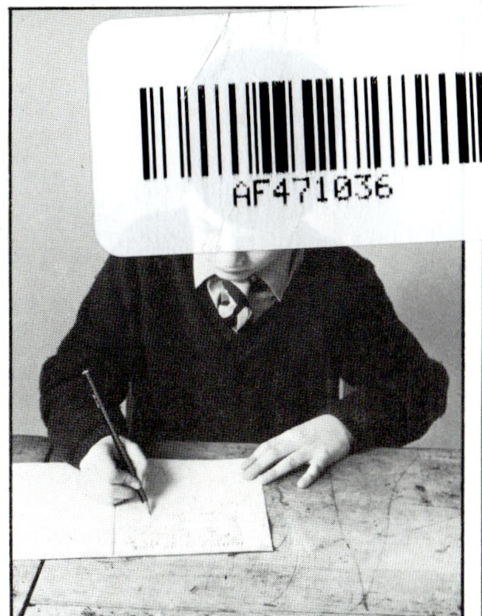

Do these exercises many times moving your pencil quickly and lightly:

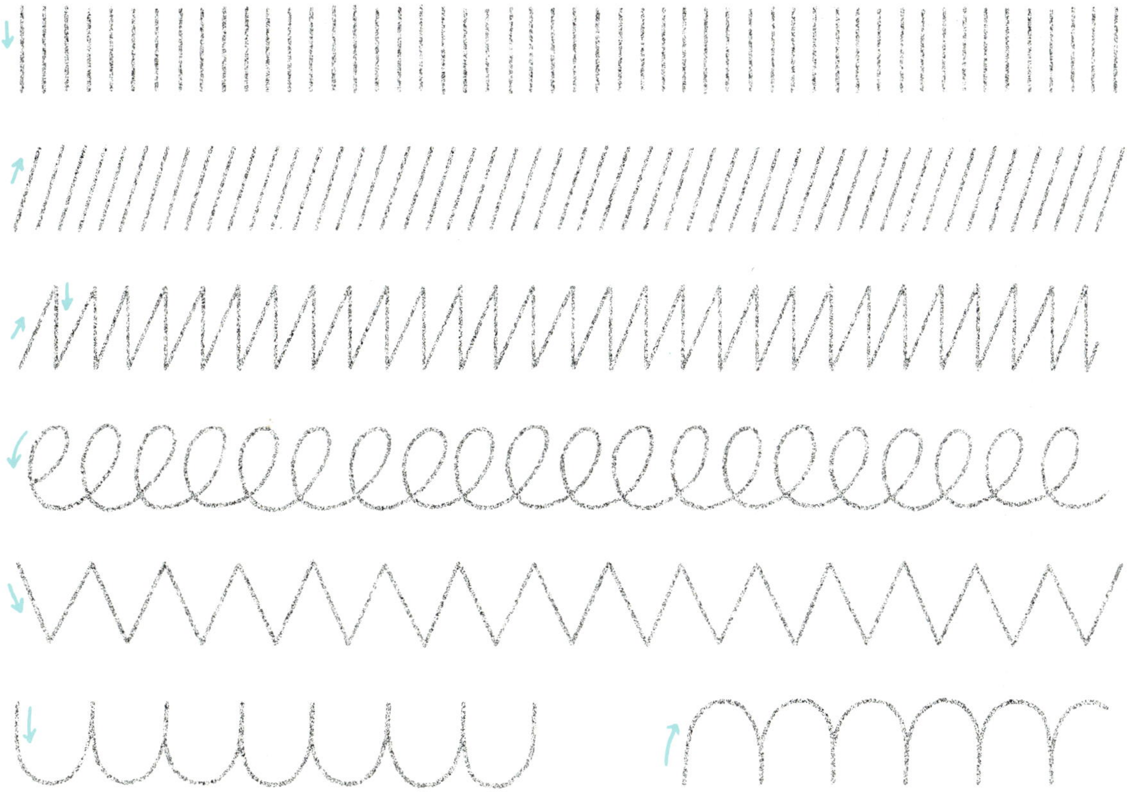

Practise all the print script letters and numerals. Make sure you can do them well.

f i j k l t z

v w x y

b h m n p r

s u

a c d e g o q

A B C D E F G H I J

K L M N O P Q R S

T U V W X Y Z

0 1 2 3 4

5 6 7 8 9

Compare the two sentences below but do not copy them. What differences do you notice? The first is written in Nelson Infant Writing, the second in Nelson joined. In this book you will be starting to learn joined writing.

At exactly six o'clock the quiet of the airport was shattered as five big jet planes zoomed by.

At exactly six o'clock the quiet of the airport was shattered as five big jet planes zoomed by.

Look back at the second example of joined writing on page 3 and see how the 26 lower case letters are used in Nelson joined writing. Some of the basic letter shapes are different from Nelson Infant Writing.

Look at these letters used in Nelson joined:

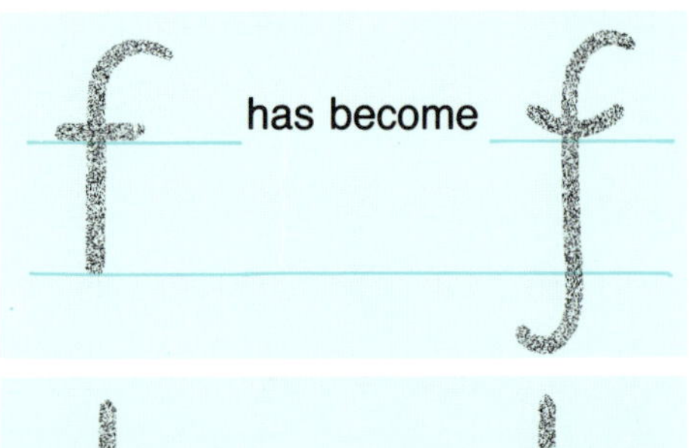

f   has become   f   Its tail does not descend as far as the tail of y.
It is not as tall as k .

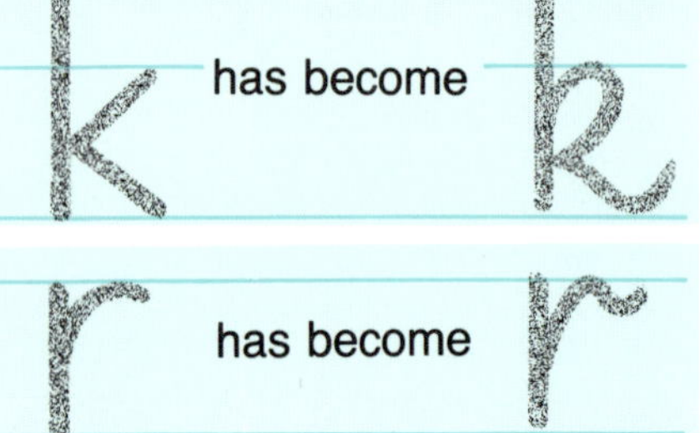

k   has become   k   It has a kink in its tail so that it can be made in one continuous movement.

r   has become   r   Its tail has an extra little curve at the top for easy joining.

y   has become   y   The y has a curved tail.

Now practise these letters until you can write them easily and well:

f f f f f f f f f f f f

k k k k k k k k k k k k

r r r r r r r r r r r r

y y y y y y y y y y y y

Twelve of the letters used in Nelson joined script end with a little curved up-stroke. They are:

a c d e h i

k l m n t u

Another eleven remain the same as in Nelson Infant Writing. They are:

b g j o p q s v w x z

Pay special attention to the new letter shapes:

f k r y

All letters except f i j t x are made without lifting your pencil from the paper.

Practise making all the letters until you can write them easily and well:

a b c d e f g h i j k

l m n o p q r s t u v

w x y z

It is important that all letters are made the right size. Letters with ascenders (tall letters) should be almost twice as tall as ordinary letters. Letters with descenders (letters with tails) should be not quite twice as long as ordinary ones. Capital letters are the same size as tall letters.

Ordinary letters (no ascenders or descenders)

a c e i m n o r s

u v w x z

Letters with ascenders (tall letters)

b d f h k l t

Letters with descenders (letters with tails)

g j p q y

Capital letters (These are the same size as tall letters.)

A B C D E F G H   b d

I J K L M N O   h l

P Q R S T U V   k d

W X Y Z   h b

These three words are written in Nelson joined writing. Look carefully at the way they are joined:

ace name and

Notice how the curved up-stroke from the *a* of *ace* continues to the beginning of the *c*. This is the same as the rising part of the swings pattern you have practised so often.

The up-swing is the basic join so you should practise this pattern until you can make it smoothly and easily:

To help us think about joins we can sort the letters into sets. The 12 letters which, like *a*, end with a little curved up-stroke at 6 o'clock, are Set 1. Practise the Set 1 letters until you can write them easily and well.

a c d e h i k l m n t u

The up-stroke starts here:

Set 2 is the group of letters without left-side ascenders which start at either twelve or one o'clock. There are 19 letters in Set 2. Practise the Set 2 letters many times also.

They start here:

a c d e g i j m n o p

q r s u v w x y

The two letters which form the word *in* are written together without stopping or lifting the pencil. Trace over this word many times with the blunt end of your pencil. Dot the *i* after the word is finished.

Practise this pattern again for the basic join:

Write a row like this slowly and carefully. Do not lift your pencil between the beginning and ending of a word.

in   in   in   in   in   in   in   in

Now write a row more quickly but still keeping the right joins and the correct spaces between the letters. Practise this until you can do it easily and well.

in   in   in   in   in   in   in   in

Try the same two letters in these words:

din   tin   din   tin   din   tin

Here is another join for you to trace and practise:

im   im   im   im   im

aim   dim   aim   dim

him   him   him   him   him

iniminim   iniminim   iniminim

Look carefully at these joins. Trace over them with the blunt end of your pencil.

ip aj am an

Now practise these examples:

ip ip ip ip ip ip ip ip ip

dip hip lip nip tip

aj aj aj aj aj aj aj aj aj aj

ajar major majesty

am am am an an an

cam dam man pan tan

an an an an ap ap ap ap

can pan man lap nap tap

Trace over these joins with the blunt end of your pencil:

cu   dr   ey   iv

Practise these examples:

cu cu cu cu cu cu cu

cud cup cur cure curl

dr dr dr dr dr dr dr

draw dream drop dry

ew ew ew iv iv iv

dew jewel live river new

ey ey ey ey ey ey ey

drey grey prey obey

Trace over these joins with the blunt end of your pencil:

ho la ma na

Practise these examples:

ho ho ho ho no no no no

hole home hot north now

la la la la la la la la

lace lamp land lap late

ma ma ma ma ma ma

mad made mark mat may

no no no no ta ta ta ta ta

now none north tail tar tap

The Set 1 letters all finish with a curved up-stroke:

a c d e h i k l m n t u

Look carefully at how Set 1 letters join to _e_ :

dine ten meet

The up-swing of the basic join forms the lower part of the letter _e_ as well as making the join.

Join _e_ together a number of times like this. Notice its shape.

eeeeeee   eeeeeeee   eeeeeee

When you can make them easily and well practise joins from other Set 1 letters to _e_.

ae   ce   de   ee   he   ie   ke   le

me   ne   te   ue

Now try these words:

aeroplane face din deed

heel lie cake tale came

dine tent blue

On page 21 you will learn about a slightly different _e_

The letter S in print script is always the same rounded snake shape:

In Nelson joined writing there is a change of shape when S comes after a join. Look carefully at these words:

bus case dish

Because the up-swing of the basic join comes up to the beginning of the S diagonally, it makes the S more pointed at the top.

Practise making joins to S after all the relevant Set 1 letters. Write them many times until you can do it easily and well:

as ds es is ks ls ms as

ns ts us as ds es is ns

Now try these words:

last   rods   toes   sister

rocks   meals   prams   buns

hats   must

On page 22 you will learn about a slightly different S

The swings pattern helps with the basic join so practise it often:

We have learned to use the basic join to join Set 1 letters to Set 2 letters. Some letters occur in both sets and can be joined together without a break. They are:

i a c d e m n u

Practise writing the words below which are all made up from the eight letters above. Take care to get your ascenders and descenders the right height.

ace acid aim cad came

mend day mind age

acid game dim again

cane dame den dice

dime din dine in mane

mean men mend mice

mind mine mud name nun

The second join to learn is the one from letters in Set 1 (*a c d e h i k l m n t u*) to letters in Set 3, which have ascenders on the left hand side. The Set 3 letters are:

b   f   h   k   l   t

Notice that this join is not made to the top of the letter *b* but to a point roughly half-way up. The join is still made by continuing the curved up-stroke from *a* until it meets *b* . The pencil continues to the top of the ascender, then down to the bottom, then up and round to form the bowl of the *b* . The swings pattern is the basis of this join too.

First practise the swings pattern a few times:

Now practise writing *ab* correctly joined until you can write it quickly, easily and well:

ab   ab   ab   ab   ab   ab   ab

Now try *eb*

eb   eb   eb   eb   eb   eb   eb

And *ub*

ub   ub   ub   ub   ub   ub   ub

And *ib*

ib   ib   ib   ib   ib   ib   ib

Remember to dot the *i* after you have finished.

Practise these examples:

ch ch ch ch ch ch ch ch

th th th th th th th th

ak ak ak ak ak ak ak ak

ck ck ck ck ck ck ck ck

ek ek ek ek ek ek ek ek

lk lk lk lk lk lk lk lk

uk uk uk uk uk uk uk uk

al al al al al al al al

el el el el el el el el

il il il il il il il il

ll ll ll ll ll ll ll ll

ul ul ul ul ul ul ul ul

You have practised joining the Set 1 letters to some of the Set 3 letters (b h k l). However, you may find that joins from Set 1 letters to ƒ and t need a lot more practice.

This is how the joins are made:

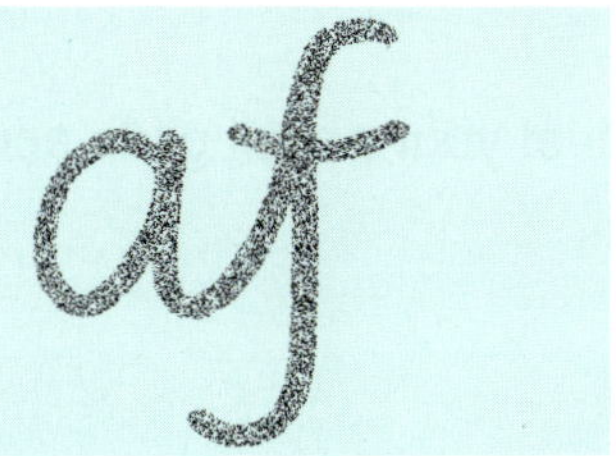

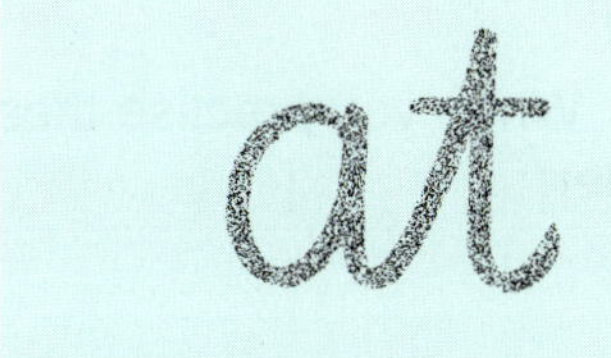

Practise writing the letters on their own and be sure you can write them quickly and easily. Remember that t and ƒ are not as tall as the other letters with ascenders.

ƒ ƒ ƒ ƒ ƒ ƒ ƒ ƒ ƒ ƒ ƒ ƒ

t t t t t t t t t t t t

Practise the swings pattern again:

Now practise these joins:

af af af af af af af

at at at at at at at

af at af at af at af

Check back to page 1:
● Are you sitting correctly?   ● Are you holding your pencil correctly but lightly?   ● Is your paper placed correctly on the table?

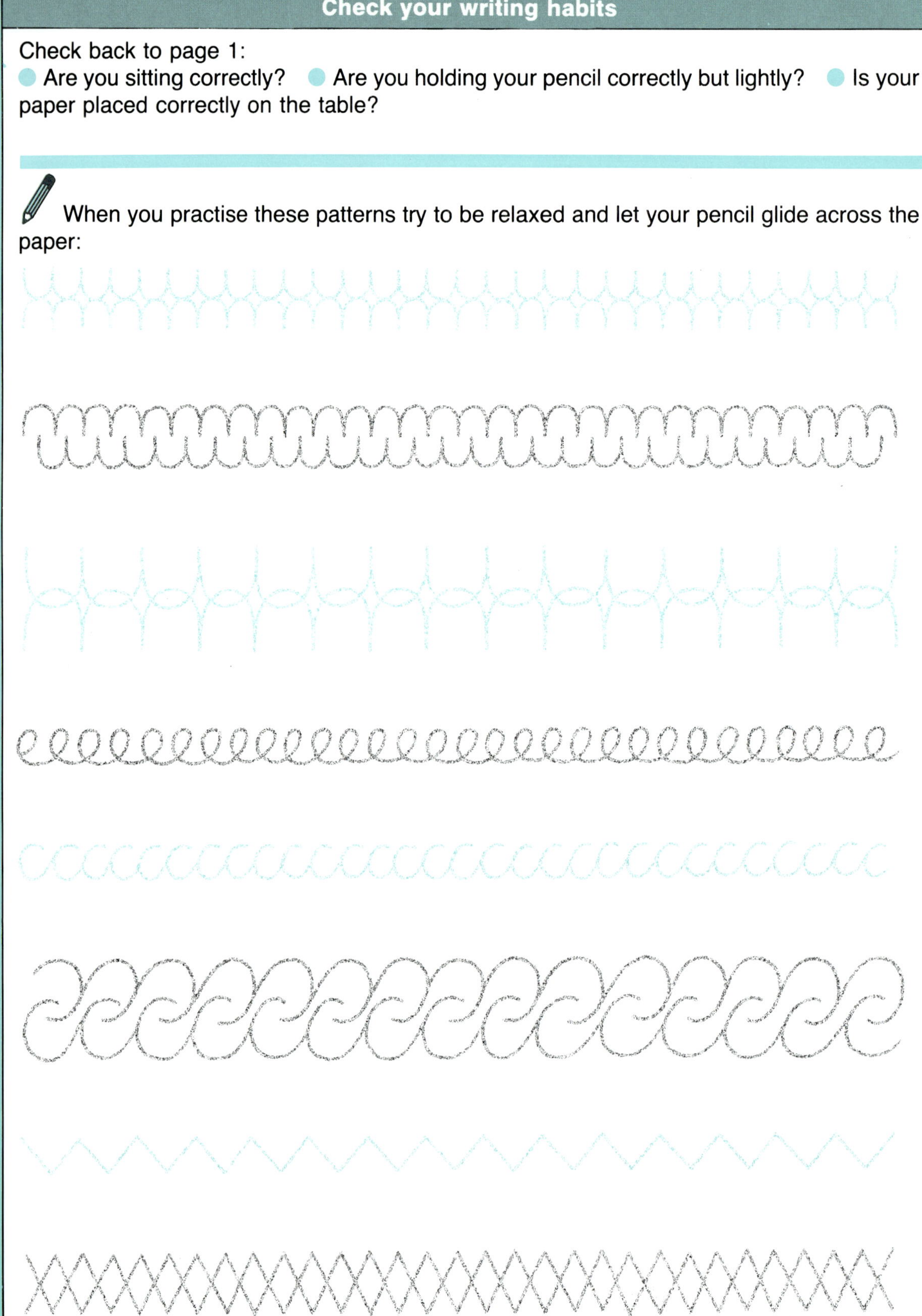

When you practise these patterns try to be relaxed and let your pencil glide across the paper:

The joins you have learned so far have been made from Set 1 letters which end with a curved up-stroke at the bottom. A different join is used when we join Set 4 letters to Set 2 letters.

The Set 4 letters are:

f   o   r   v   w

Remember that the Set 2 letters are:

a   c   d   e   g   i   j   m   n   o

p   q   r   s   u   v   w   y   x

The join is a shallow horizontal curve. It must be the right length to keep the space between letters the same as with the basic and second joins.

oa

Practise *oa* correctly until you can write it easily and well:

oa   oa   oa   oa   oa   oa   oa

Now practise these examples:

oa   oa   oa   oa   oa   oa   oa

oi   oi   oi   oi   oi   oi   oi

og   og   og   og   og   og   og

om   om   om   om   om   om   om

Practise these examples:

fa fa fa fa fa fa fa fa

rc rc rc rc rc rc rc rc

rd rd rd rd rd rd rd rd

rn rn rn rn rn rn rn rn

rp rp rp rp rp rp rp rp

wa wa wa wa wa wa

oc oc oc oc oc oc

vo vo vo vo vo vo

vu vu vu vu vu vu

wi wi wi wi wi wi

wr wr wr wr wr wr

On page 12 we learned that when *e* is joined on from a letter in Set 1 the bowl of the *e* slopes diagonally, like this:

Look carefully at what happens in these two examples of *e* following a Set 4 letter. The bowl of letter *e* is more horizontal. The joins are shallow horizontal curves.

Practise these joins:

Practise these patterns:

On page 13 we learned that when s is joined on from a letter in Set 1 the s becomes more pointed at the top:

Look carefully at what happens in these two examples of s following a Set 4 letter. The top of the s becomes flatter. The joins are shallow horizontal curves.

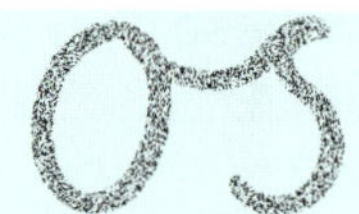

Practise these joins:

Practise these patterns:

The fourth and last join to learn is the one from Set 4 letters (*f o r v w*) to Set 3 (*b f h k l t*).

Once again the join is the same as the up-swing in the swings pattern but this time the join travels from the top of the Set 4 letter towards the top of the ascender of the Set 3 letter:

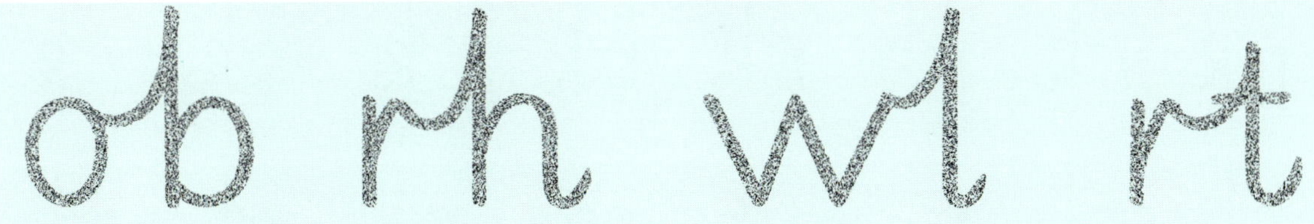

Practise these joins:

ob   ob   ob   ob   ob   ob

of   of   of   of   of   of

ot   ot   ot   ot   ot   ot

oh   oh   oh   oh   oh   oh

ol   ol   ol   ol   ol   ol

ok   ok   ok   ok   ok   ok

Practise these joins:

rb rb rb rb rb rb rb rb

rk rk rk rk rk rk rk rk

rl rl rl rl rl rl rl rl

rt rt rt rt rt rt rt rt

wk wk wk wk wk

wt wt wt wt wt wt

fl fl fl fl fl fl

ft ft ft ft ft ft

Pay special attention to joining one *f* to another. From the bar of the first *f* a join is made to the top of the second *f* :

ff ff ff ff ff

ff ff ff ff ff

There are 9 letters *after* which a join is not made:

b g j p q s x y z

No joins are ever made *to* z either.

Practise writing these words. Take care over all the joins. Leave a small space after the break letters so that they are spaced as regularly as the joined letters.

bigger bigger bigger bigger

just just just just

queen queen queen queen

zebra zebra zebra zebra

pistol pistol pistol pistol

boss boss boss boss

stable stable stable stable

boxer boxer boxer boxer

Practise all the joins below many times. If you have any difficulty go back to the pages where they were introduced.

Basic join (Pages 7–14)

mi ac ue ds ko mi ac

Second join (Pages 15–17)

ib nh ck ef al ib

Third join (Pages 18–22)

fa rm fe ws va fa

Fourth join (Pages 23–24)

rl ot wk ft rk rl

No join (Page 25)

go ba uz ze ji go

Now practise writing this sentence several times. Start off writing it slowly and carefully, checking that all your letters and joins are made properly. Then try to speed up without making mistakes.

A quick brown fox jumps over the lazy dog.

 Practise making patterns like these quickly and well:

The capital letters for Nelson joined writing are exactly the same as for Nelson books A and B. Turn to page 2 and practise making all the capital letters several times each.

Capital letters are never joined to the other letters in a word. We use capital letters to begin proper names. Practise writing the following words which all begin with capital letters:

Ann Balvinder Carol

Dan Edward Fred Grace

Helen Iris John Kate Lucy

Mary Nadeem Olive Peter

Queenie Ranjit Sara Tom

Una Victor Wendy Yvonne

Check that you have made all letters and joins correctly.

 Practise these numbers until you can write them quickly and well:

1 2 3 4 5 6 7 8 9 0

Now practise writing all the numbers from 1 to 30 as quickly as you can but being sure to write them well. Time yourself and repeat the experiment several times, trying to improve your speed.

When you set down sums be sure to make your figures clear and arrange them in straight lines. Copy down these addition and subtraction sums and work out the answers. Be sure your figures are well made.

Addition

$$
\begin{array}{r} 13 \\ 24 \\ +42 \\ \hline \end{array}
\qquad
\begin{array}{r} 27 \\ 38 \\ +14 \\ \hline \end{array}
\qquad
\begin{array}{r} 43 \\ 16 \\ +27 \\ \hline \end{array}
\qquad
\begin{array}{r} 29 \\ 35 \\ +38 \\ \hline \end{array}
$$

Subtraction

$$
\begin{array}{r} 69 \\ -34 \\ \hline \end{array}
\qquad
\begin{array}{r} 87 \\ -25 \\ \hline \end{array}
\qquad
\begin{array}{r} 93 \\ -14 \\ \hline \end{array}
\qquad
\begin{array}{r} 75 \\ -48 \\ \hline \end{array}
$$

Using a three minute timer, see how many times you can manage to write this pattern of numbers. Again make sure all your figures are well made.

1 2 3 4 5 6 7 8 9 0

9 8 7 6 5 4 3 2 1 0

The words in each set below have something in common. Can you spot the connection? Discuss this with your teacher. Write out each set and also write your explanation.

Check your writing to see that all your letters and joins are properly made.

Set 1

enormous

large

colossal

huge

gigantic

Set 2

wheel

brake

gear

clutch

windscreen

Set 3

jump

walk

dance

skate

sing

Set 4

mum

radar

peep

madam

Set 5

ugly

clean

shiny

pretty

Set 6

hollow

glimmer

llama

cannon

Write out this rhyme carefully. Check that you have made all letters and joins correctly.

Solomon Grundy
Born on Monday
Christened on Tuesday
Married on Wednesday
Took ill on Thursday
Worse on Friday
Died on Saturday
Buried on Sunday
That is the end of
Solomon Grundy

When you write out this rhyme give extra thought to the way you make your ascenders and descenders.

playing   heard   spoke

Remember, the ascenders and descenders should not quite reach to the lines above or below.

There was an old owl
who lived in an oak,
The more he heard the
less he spoke.
The less he spoke, the
more he heard.
Why aren't we like
that wise old bird?

Check through your writing of this rhyme and see that all letters and joins are properly made. Pay particular attention to the proportions of ascenders and descenders.

 First write this carefully in your best writing:

Autumn

Yellow the bracken,
Golden the sheaves,
Rosy the apples,
Crimson the leaves:
Mist on the hillside
Clouds grey and white,
Autumn, good morning!
Summer, good night!

Look carefully at what you have written. Check letter shapes and sizes, check the joins and check the spaces between letters, words and lines.

Now try writing the poem well but quickly. Check again for mistakes.